EARTHQUAKES

EARTHQUAKES

By Franklyn M. Branley

Illustrated by Megan Lloyd

HarperCollins Publishers

The *Let's-Read-and-Find-Out Science* book series was originated by Dr. Franklyn M. Branley, Astronomer Emeritus and former Chairman of the American Museum–Hayden Planetarium, and was formerly co-edited by him and Dr. Roma Gans, Professor Emeritus of Childhood Education, Teachers College, Columbia University. Text and illustrations for each of the books in the series are checked for accuracy by an expert in the relevant field. For more information about Let's-Read-and-Find-Out Science books, write to HarperCollins Children's Books, 10 East 53rd Street, New York, NY 10022, or visit our website at www.letsreadandfindout.com.

Library of Congress Cataloging-in-Publication Data
Branley, Franklyn Mansfield.
  Earthquakes / by Franklyn M. Branley ; illustrated by Megan Lloyd.— Newly illustrated ed.
    p. cm. — (Let's-read-and-find-out science. Stage 2)
  ISBN 0-06-028008-5 — ISBN 0-06-028009-3 (lib. bdg.) — ISBN 0-06-445188-7 (pbk.)
  1. Earthquakes—Juvenile literature. [1. Earthquakes.] I. Lloyd, Megan, ill. II. Title. III. Series.
QE521.3.B72 2005   2003025458
551.22—dc22   CIP
                                                                                                        AC

Typography by Elynn Cohen 13 LP 20 19 18 17 16 15 14 13 12 11   ❖   Newly Illustrated Edition

To Karen and Fred,
who live where it might shake
but, hopefully, won't.
Love,
M.L.

Parts of the earth are always moving. That's hard to believe, but they are. The movements are so small and so slow, we usually cannot feel them.

Whole mountains move. Big sections of a continent like North America can move. Even whole continents move. Right now North America and Europe are moving apart. They move slowly, only as fast as your fingernails grow. So we don't feel the motion.

6

When parts of the earth move quickly, there may be an earthquake. Every day there are at least a thousand earthquakes on our planet. Most are small, but each year there are a few earthquakes large enough to knock down buildings.

The strength of an earthquake can be measured. We use something called the Richter scale, named after C. F. Richter, an American scientist. Anything that measures less than 2 is a small quake, and 8 or higher is a very big one.

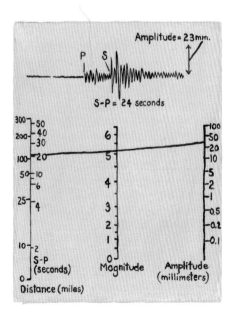

Every earthquake has a center. That's where it all begins.
Parts of the earth move up and down or sideways and make
waves that spread out and go through the whole earth.

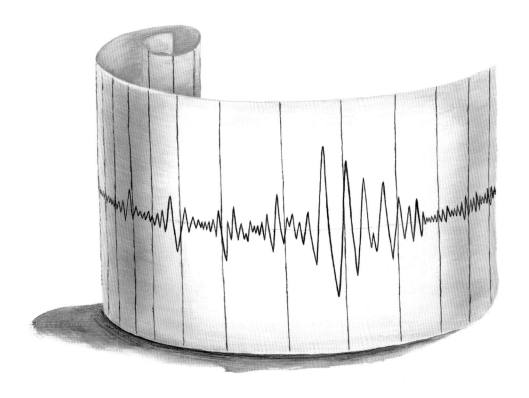

They are called seismic waves. The word comes from *seismos*, a Greek word meaning to shake. Scientists all over the world measure the waves on seismometers.

Here is an experiment to help you understand how waves work. Hold a yardstick near your ear. Have someone tap lightly on the other end. You can hear the sound clearly because a wave went through the yardstick. Waves travel through rock the way sound travels through wood.

There are also up-and-down waves, like the waves in a rope when you flip it up and down. This kind of wave also goes through the earth.

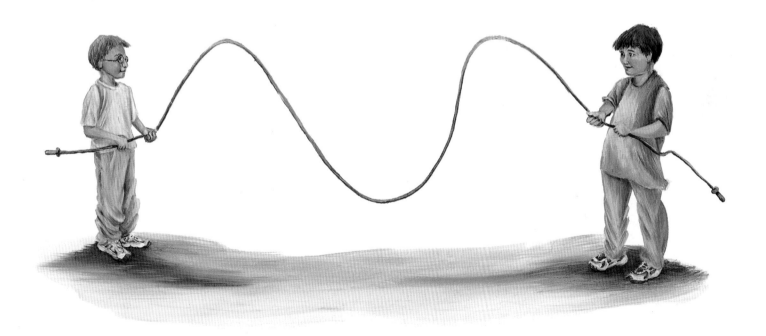

We live on the outer part of Earth. It is called Earth's crust. In some places the crust is 30 or 40 miles thick. If Earth were an apple, the crust would be only as thick as the skin of the apple. Most earthquakes occur in the crust.

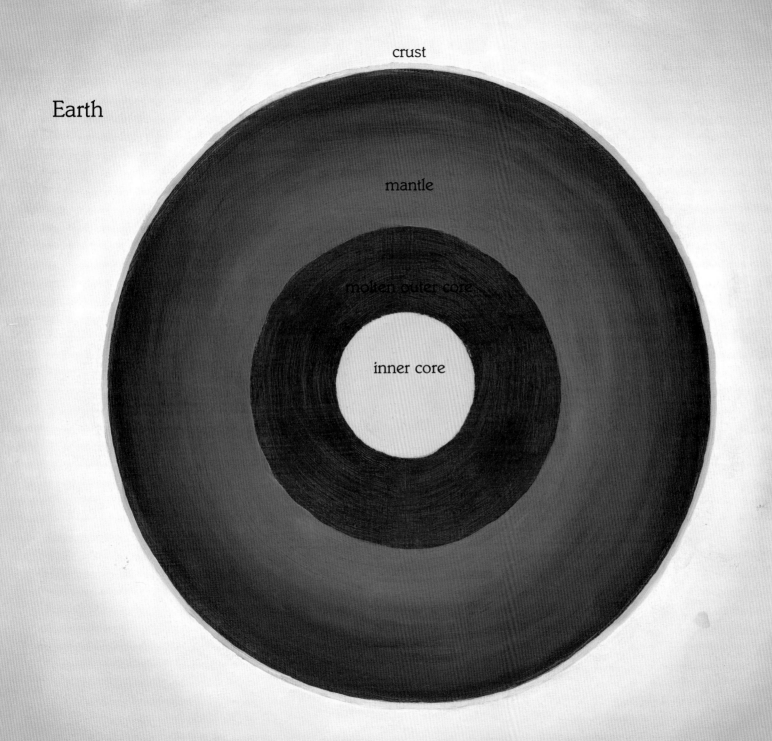

Earth

crust

mantle

molten outer core

inner core

13

Large sections of the earth's crust are always moving. Sometimes two sections push against each other. The place where they meet is called a fault. When the sections cannot pass, the earth bends and buckles. Suddenly the bend releases, and a whole section may move four or five feet at once.

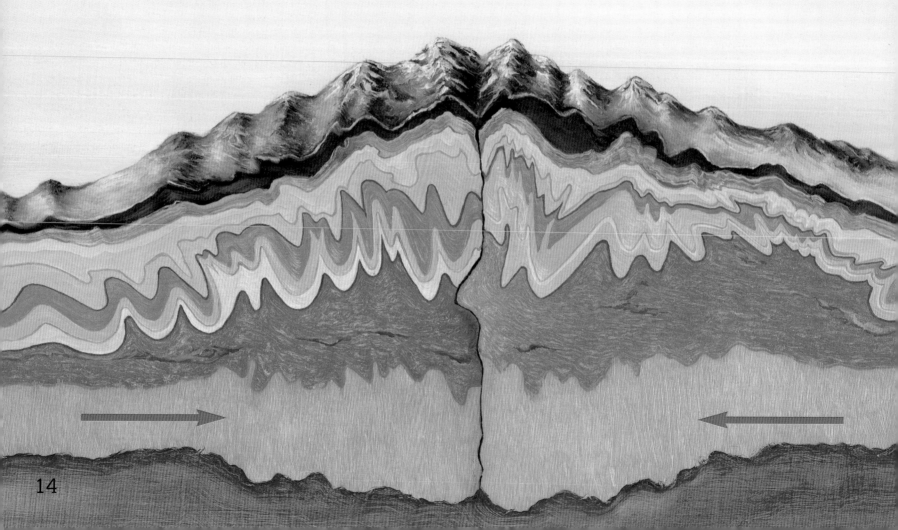

That's what happened twelve miles below the surface of Mexico in 1985. The seismic waves from the earthquake's center were strong enough to topple buildings in Mexico City, 220 miles away, and kill several thousand people. The quake measured 8.1 on the Richter scale.

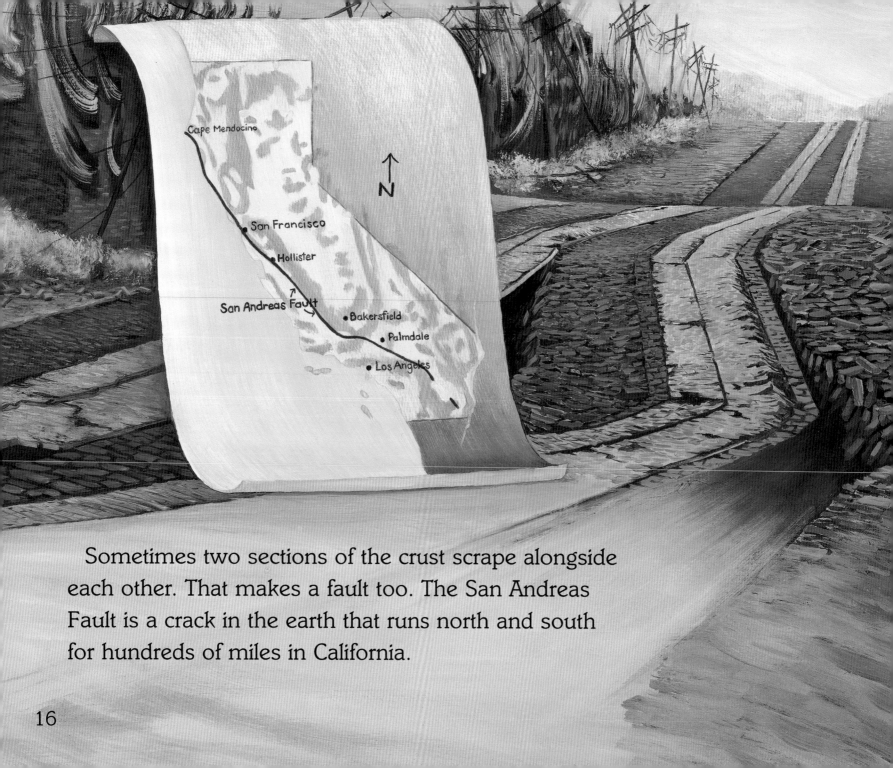

Sometimes two sections of the crust scrape alongside each other. That makes a fault too. The San Andreas Fault is a crack in the earth that runs north and south for hundreds of miles in California.

In 1906 there was an earthquake along a section of the San Andreas Fault. In seconds, the crust on the west side of the fault moved twenty feet. San Francisco and the area around the city shook and trembled. Fires started, and most of the city burned down.

17

Most earthquakes occur along the shores of the Pacific Ocean, where the crust moves a lot. Japan has about 7,000 earthquakes a year. Luckily, most are small.

There are volcanoes in this part of the world too. Earthquakes often occur in places where there are volcanoes. Melted rock deep under the earth pushes upward, making the area shake and rumble. These are warnings that a volcano may erupt or that there may be a big earthquake.

In southern Europe there are several volcanoes. There are also many earthquakes. In Pozzuoli, Italy, a small town not far from Mount Vesuvius, there were 4,000 quakes in one year. Mount Vesuvius is a volcano that has erupted from time to time for several thousand years.

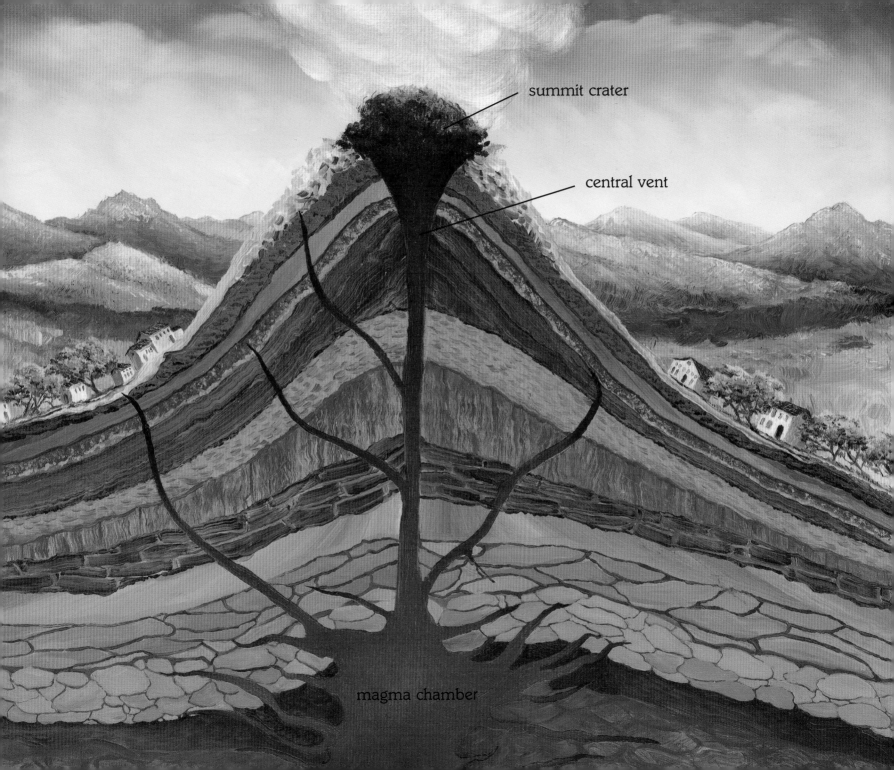

summit crater

central vent

magma chamber

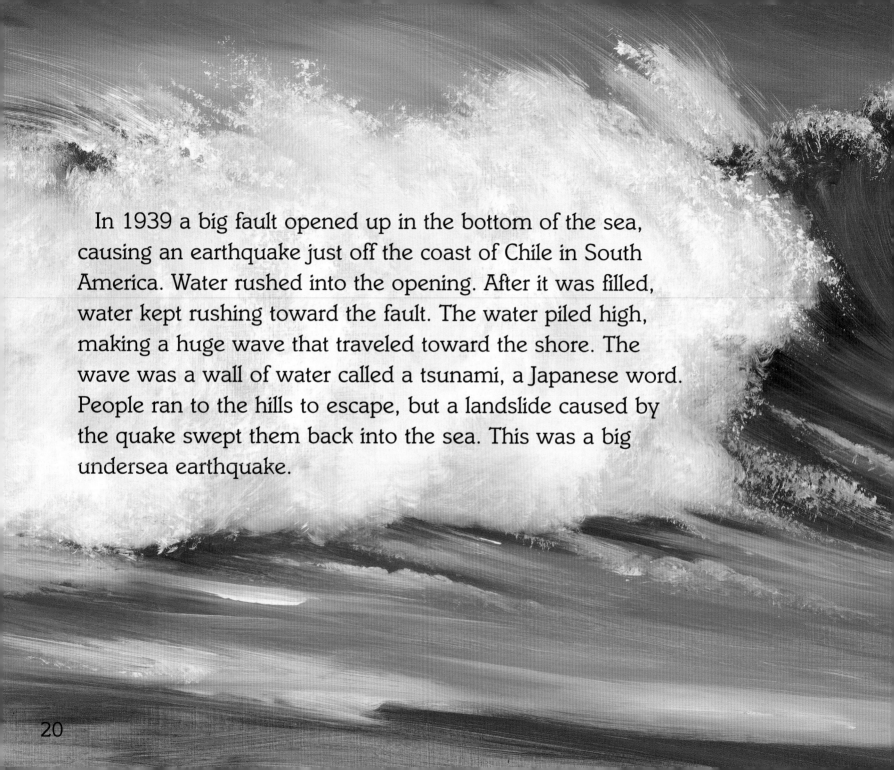

In 1939 a big fault opened up in the bottom of the sea, causing an earthquake just off the coast of Chile in South America. Water rushed into the opening. After it was filled, water kept rushing toward the fault. The water piled high, making a huge wave that traveled toward the shore. The wave was a wall of water called a tsunami, a Japanese word. People ran to the hills to escape, but a landslide caused by the quake swept them back into the sea. This was a big undersea earthquake.

21

In a small quake, dishes rattle. Ceiling lights swing. The ground jiggles a bit as if a big truck were going by. It's all over in a few seconds.

22

During a big earthquake, many buildings fall down. There are also fires. Pipes that carry gas to homes are broken. A spark may set the gas afire. Sometimes firefighters can't fight the flames because water pipes have been broken.

During an earthquake, dams may break too. Rivers may be blocked by landslides. So there is often flooding in the area of an earthquake.

In many parts of the world where there are big earthquakes, new buildings are made of steel instead of wood. They are built where the ground is solid so seismic waves will not knock them down. Old bridges and dams are made stronger with extra steel and concrete.

In 1989, there was a serious earthquake near San Francisco. It was the worst in the area since 1906. Sixty-seven people were killed. Bridges and roadways were damaged, and many buildings were destroyed. Because of the way it was built, the famous Golden Gate Bridge swayed in the quake, but it did not collapse.

Earthquakes happen without any warning. However, scientists are working to find ways to predict quakes. They use satellites to measure even the smallest motion along faults. These small motions can often become larger.

It is important to know what to do in case of an earthquake. If you are outside, stay away from buildings, trees, power lines, or anything else that could fall on you. If you can, go to an open space, like a ball field or parking lot.

If you are inside, stay there. Get under a strong table or bed, or stand in a doorway. Keep away from windows.

If you are in school, your teacher will tell you what to do.

Wherever you are, remember there may be smaller shocks after the main quake. These aftershocks could cause more damage.

People who live in places where there have been earthquakes should always keep a supply of plastic bottles of drinking water. They should also have a supply of canned food, a flashlight, a fire extinguisher, and a battery-powered radio.

The crust of our planet is always moving, so we will continue to have earthquakes. Most of them, fortunately, will be small ones.

We hope there is never a big earthquake near you. But if there is, you know there are things that you can do to protect yourself and other people.

Earthquake Facts

- The strongest earthquake since 1900 occurred in Chile in 1960, with a magnitude of 9.5.
- Antarctica is the continent with the lowest number of recorded earthquakes.
- Even though many people believe that animals have a "sixth sense" when it comes to natural disasters like earthquakes, there is no scientific proof that this is true.
- The moon experiences tremors much like the earth does—"moonquakes"! They occur less frequently than quakes do on earth, and farther below the surface.
- Many famous writers and scientists have written about earthquakes. Mark Twain wrote about the San Francisco earthquake of 1865, and Jack London wrote about the San Francisco earthquake of 1906 for *Collier's* magazine. Charles Darwin wrote to friends about what he saw in the 1835 earthquake in Chile.
- Immediately after an earthquake, the water in the ponds, lakes, and pools of the area will slosh back and forth for a short period of time in reaction to the force of the quake. This is called a seiche (pronounced *saysh*). This effect isn't always limited to the earthquake's immediate area. In 1985, the University of Arizona's pool lost water due to the 8.1 magnitude quake in Mexico.
- Only four states did not have any earthquakes from 1975 to 1995: Florida, Iowa, North Dakota, and Wisconsin.

The Top Ten Most Destructive Earthquakes (in terms of lives lost)

1. China   1/23/1556   Magnitude of 8   830,000 deaths

2. China   7/27/1976   Magnitude of 7.5   255,000 deaths

3. Syria   8/9/1136   Unknown magnitude   230,000 deaths

4. China   5/22/1927   Magnitude of 7.9   200,000 deaths

5. Iran   12/22/856   Unknown magnitude   200,000 deaths

6. China   12/16/1920 Magnitude of 8.6   200,000 deaths

7. Iran   3/23/893   Unknown magnitude   150,000 deaths

8. Japan   9/1/1923   Magnitude of 7.9   143,000 deaths

9. Turkmenistan   10/5/1948   Magnitude of 7.3   110,000 deaths

10. Italy   12/28/1908 Magnitude of 7.2   70,000 to 100,000 deaths

For more information visit http://neic.usgs.gov/neis/eqlists/eqsmosde.html.